T0151424

dim sum

by Vicki Liley

TUTTLE Publishing

Tokyo | Rutland, Vermont | Singapore

Published by Tuttle Publishing, an imprint of Periplus
Editions (HK) Ltd.

www.tuttlepublishing.com

ISBN: 978-0-8048-3844-3
Printed in Malaysia

Distributed by
USA
Tuttle Publishing, 364 Innovation Drive,
North Clarendon, VT 05759-9436 U.S.A.
Tel: 1 (802) 773-8930 Fax: 1 (802) 773-6993
info@tuttlepublishing.com
www.tuttlepublishing.com

Japan
Tuttle Publishing, Yaekari Building, 3rd Floor,
5-4-12 Osaki, Shinagawa-ku, Tokyo 141 0032.
Tel. (81) 3 5437-0171 Fax. (81) 3 5437-0755
www.tuttle.co.jp

Asia Pacific
Berkeley Books Pte. Ltd..
61 Tai Seng Avenue, #02-12
Singapore 534167
Tel: (65) 6280-1330 Fax: (65) 6280-6290
inquiries@periplus.com.sg
www.periplus.com

12 11 10
7 6 5 4 3

Contents

Serving Dim Sum

A Cantonese specialty, dim sum (variously translated as "dot hearts," "heart warmers" and "heart's delight") is the collective name for a variety of small, delicious snacks. It includes steamed or fried dumplings with meat or seafood fillings, steamed buns, shrimp balls and always a few desserts.

It is the Chinese custom to enjoy these tiny morsels with a pot or two of Chinese tea. Dim sum, or *yum cha*, as it is sometimes known, has become a tradition on Sunday mornings in most cities with a sizeable Chinese population. The little delicacies are displayed on trays and trolleys which pass by your table, tempting you to try them. Some trolleys are stacked with steaming buns in bamboo steamers, others with hot fried spring rolls and other "wrapped" dishes. The trolleys are brought around constantly so you need take only one or two dishes at a time and enjoy them when they're freshly cooked.

At home, dim sum is a different story: you can't possibly make the huge selection available to you in a restaurant. Instead choose two or three different dishes—most recipes can be prepared ahead of time, leaving the steaming or frying to be done at the last minute. All you need in the way of equipment is a wok and a bamboo steamer or two. Dim sum dishes can't be left sitting around: hot dishes should be served as hot as possible, and many are accompanied by soy sauce, chili sauce or one of the special dipping sauces on pages 16 to 17.

One or two dim sum dishes make an elegant and surprising appetizer to serve with drinks before dinner, and it is exceptional cocktail food (for a cocktail party of any size, you'll need a helper in the kitchen to keep the food coming). If you are serving a dim sum brunch, allow 8 to 10 bite-sized pieces per person and serve the food on small plates or in the steamers in which they are cooked. Set each place with a small bowl and chopsticks. Serve with Chinese tea.

Drinking Tea

Chinese legend has it that, in 2737 b.c., the Emperor Chen-Nung discovered tea by accident while sipping boiled water in his garden one day. A few leaves fell from a tea bush into his cup, the emperor tasted it and liked it, and the tea drinking custom began.

By the fourth century a.d., tea was firmly established in China and was thought to have medicinal and restorative powers. The eighth-century poet Lu Yu wrote in the Cha King, or Holy Scripture of Tea, the first book ever written about tea, "... tea tempers the spirits, calms and harmonises the mind; it arouses thought and prevents drowsiness, lightens and refreshes the body, and clears the perceptive faculties."

Chinese tea is always served and consumed with dim sum. Milk or sugar is never added. When making Chinese tea, always select good-quality tea leaves and use only freshly boiled water. Traditionally, the Chinese use porcelain teapots and tiny porcelain cups without handles. Good teas can be infused three times—the second time is generally regarded as the best because, by then, the tea will release its full fragrance and aroma. About 1 teaspoon of tea is used to make one cup.

Chinese tea may be classified into five varieties: scented, black, green, white and Oolong.

Scented tea Made from green tea, which is fully dried, then lightly scented with fragrant flowers. Scented tea is named after the flower with which it is scented—jasmine, orange bud, rose bud or white chrysanthemum.

Black tea Fully fermented tea. The leaves turn black during the fermentation process.

Green tea Manufactured without going through the process of fermentation. The natural emerald green color of the leaves is preserved.

White tea A rare unfermented tea. The name "white" comes from the silvery-white color of the leaves.

Oolong tea A semi-fermented tea combining the aromas and flavors of both green and black teas.

Equipment and Utensils

A wok is the perfect size and shape for steaming and deep-frying dim sum recipes. Carbon steel or rolled steel woks, the popular inexpensive vessels you see in Asian stores, are coated with a thin film of lacquer to prevent rusting. The film needs to be removed before the wok can be used. The best way to do this is to place the wok on the stove top, fill with cold water and add 2 tablespoons baking soda (bicarbonate of soda). Bring to the boil and boil rapidly for 15 minutes. Drain and scrub off the coating with a nylon pad. Repeat the process if any coating remains. Then rinse and dry the wok. It is now ready to be seasoned.

Carbon steel, rolled steel and cast-iron woks require seasoning before use, which creates a smooth surface that keeps food from sticking to it and prevents it from discoloring. To season a wok, place over low heat. Have paper towels and vegetable oil handy. When the wok is hot, carefully wipe it with an oiled paper towel. Repeat the process with fresh towels until they come away clean, without any trace of color.

A seasoned wok should not be scrubbed clean with detergent after cooking. Instead, use hot water and a sponge or nylon pad. Dry the wok well after washing, heat it gently, rub it over with an oiled paper towel and store in a dry, well-ventilated place. Long periods without use can cause the oil coating on the wok to become rancid. Using your wok is the best way to prevent this from occurring.

There are a number of cooking utensils that go hand in hand with a wok. Bamboo steamers are available in many sizes at Asian supermarkets. They can be stacked on top of each other over a wok of simmering water, allowing the cook to prepare an entire meal at once or to cook the same dish in several batches. Bamboo steamers need only be rinsed in hot water after cooking. Allow them to dry thoroughly before storing. Other handy utensils are a slotted spoon or wire mesh basket for removing deep-fried foods from hot oil; a good-quality cleaver for chopping; and extra-long cooking chopsticks for stirring and lifting food.

Step-by-step Guide

Deep-frying Guide

1 Pour the required amount of oil into a large wok. Heat the oil until it reaches 375 °F (190 °C) on a deep-frying thermometer or until a small bread cube dropped in the oil sizzles and turns golden.

2 Working in batches, add food and fry until golden.

3 Use a wire mesh basket or slotted spoon to remove the food from the oil and drain on paper towels.

Steaming Guide

1 Line a bamboo steamer with parchment, or cut individual pieces of parchment for the dumplings and buns. Arrange in the steamer and cover with a lid.

2 Half fill a medium wok with water (steamer should not touch water) and bring to the boil.

3 Place the steamer in the wok and steam for the required time, adding more boiling water to the wok when necessary. Lift the steamer off the wok and carefully remove the food.

Making Dumpling

1 Place round wonton wrappers onto a work surface and cover with a damp kitchen towel. Take out one wrapper and place it on the work surface. Spoon in the filling, brush the edges with water and fold in half to form a semicircle.

2 If you have a dumpling press, working with a wrapper at a time, lay it flat in the press and spoon the filling into the center. Brush the edges of the wrapper with water. Close the press firmly to seal the edges.

3 Square or round wonton wrappers can also be formed into little pouches. Pinch the edges together to seal. Or gather the edges around the filling to form a basket, and gently squeeze the center to expose the filling at the top.

Making Buns

1 Divide the dough into walnut-sized rounds.

2 Roll or press each piece out to a circle. Cover the dough with a damp kitchen towel.

3 Working with a dough circle at a time, spoon the filling to the center. Gather the edges together and twist to seal. Cut out squares of parchment (baking paper) and place the buns onto the paper.

Essential Dim Sum Ingredients

Bok choy Asian variety of cabbage with thick, white stalks and mild-flavored, dark green leaves. Sizes of bunches vary, from longer than celery stalks to baby bok choy about 6 in (15 cm) long. Also known as flat Chinese cabbage. If unavailable, use Chinese broccoli or choy sum.

Chinese broccoli Bitter-tasting broccoli with white flowers. Also known as kailan. Chinese broccoli and choy sum can be used in place of each other.

Chinese black mushrooms

Also known as shiitake mushrooms, these intensely flavorful mushrooms are sold fresh or dried. They have a dark brown outer skin, a beige inner flesh and a slightly woody flavor. The dried mushrooms need to be rehydrated before use. Soak, off heat, in boiling water for 15 to 30 minutes and squeeze dry before slicing or chopping; discard tough stems.

Chinese cabbage Also known as Napa cabbage, this vegetable has white stems that end in tightly packed pale green leaves. It has a mild, delicate sweet taste. Chinese cabbage is available year round. Choose firm, tightly packed heads with fresh leaves.

Chinese five spice powder A ground spice mixture consisting of star anise, fennel, cloves, cinnamon and pepper. An ingredient mainly used in Chinese cooking, it is sold in small plastic packets or jars in Chinese grocery stores or the spice section of supermarkets.

Coriander leaves (cilantro) The delicate green leaves of the coriander plant which are often referred to as Chinese parsley. They have a fresh aroma and flavor and mainly used as a garnish. Italian parsley or basil may be used as a substitute, although the flavor is not the same.

Dried sweet Chinese sausages (*lap cheong*) Smoked pork sausages that are highly seasoned and slightly sweet. They are dry in texture and usually red in color, and are sold in the dry goods section of Asian butchers and supermarkets. They should be steamed for 15 minutes or baked before eating.

Choy sum Popular and widely available Chinese green vegetable with yellow flowers and thin stalks. Every part of the mild-flavored vegetable can be used. Also known as flowering cabbage.

Fish sauce A fermented fish product made by layering fish and salt in large jars and then siphoning off the liquid. It is sold bottled and is a common seasoning in Thai and Vietnamese food.

Glutinous rice A variety of rice that becomes very sticky when cooked. Mainly used in snacks, sweet and desserts. This rice must be washed thoroughly and soaked overnight before steaming. Also available as finely milled glutinous rice flour.

Hoisin sauce Sweet, thick Chinese sauce made from soybeans and also containing vinegar, sugar, chili peppers and other seasonings. It can be stored indefinitely in the refrigerator. Also called Chinese barbecue sauce.

Palm sugar A type of sugar made from the sap of the coconut or *aren* palm. It varies in color from gold to dark brown. It has a rich flavor similar to dark brown sugar, molasses or maple syrup, all of which make good substitutes. Available in Asian food stores in plastic containers or packets.

Rice paper wrappers Made from rice flour, water and salt, these brittle, paper-thin wrappers are dipped in water before being used to wrap fresh or cooked food. They are eaten raw or they can also be fried, providing a crisp and light casing.

Rice wine Sweet, low-alcohol Chinese wine, also known as Shao Xing wine or Shao Xing yellow rice wine, made from fermented glutinous rice. Sake or dry sherry can be substituted.

Sesame oil Strong-tasting oil pressed from roasted sesame seeds, mainly used as a flavoring. There is no substitute.

Spring roll wrappers Thin sheets of rice flour dough, used to enclose savory fillings. They are rolled into a cigar shape and deep-fried until golden and crisp. Sometimes called spring roll skins, they are sold frozen in the supermarket. They should be

defrosted and separated before using and covered with a damp kitchen towel while preparing.

Water chestnuts Tuber of plant grown in Asia, round in shape with subtly sweet, crunchy, light-colored flesh. Water chestnuts are widely available canned; after opening, store in clean water in the refrigerator for up to 3 weeks. Also known as horses' hooves. If unavailable, use diced celery for a texture substitute.

Wonton wrappers Thin sheets of wheat-based or egg-based dough, square or circular in shape, used to enclose a variety of fillings. Available fresh or frozen. Also called wonton skins, dumpling wrappers or *gow gees*. Fresh wrappers will keep for up to 7 days in the refrigerator. Wrappers may be frozen.

Dipping Sauces

Sweet Cilantro Dip

4 tablespoons superfine (caster) sugar
4 tablespoons water
$3/4$ cup (185 ml) white vinegar
1 small red chili pepper, deseeded and sliced
2 green onions, sliced
1 tablespoon finely chopped cilantro (coriander leaves)
$1/2$ small cucumber, deseeded and chopped

Place the sugar, water and vinegar in a small saucepan. Stir over low heat until the sugar dissolves. Remove from the heat and stir in all the other ingredients.

Makes 1 cup (250 ml)

Ginger Soy Dipping Sauce

3 teaspoons grated fresh ginger
$1/2$ cup (125 ml) soy sauce
2 tablespoons Thai sweet chili sauce

Combine all the ingredients in a small bowl and mix well.

Makes $2/3$ cup (150 ml)

Chili Sauce

2 teaspoons bottled sambal oelek (see note)
$1/2$ cup (125 ml) rice wine
1 teaspoon superfine (caster) sugar
1 tablespoon finely chopped green onions

Combine all the ingredients in a small bowl and mix well.

Note: Sambal oelek is a chili sauce consists mainly of crushed red chili peppers. It is widely used as a substitute for fresh chilies to add heat to a dish without altering its other flavors. Originated from Indonesia, it is now available in Asian food stores and large supermarkets.

Makes $1/2$ cup (125 ml)

Quick Sweet and Sour Sauce

$1^1/_2$ cups (375 ml) pineapple juice
2 tablespoons tomato ketchup
2 teaspoons tomato paste (concentrate)
2 tablespoons superfine (caster) sugar
3 tablespoons white vinegar

Place all the ingredients in a saucepan and bring to a boil. Reduce the heat to low and simmer uncovered for 10 minutes, stirring occasionally. Remove from the heat and allow to cool before serving.

Makes $1^1/_2$ cups (375 ml)

Lime and Fish Sauce

$1/_2$ cup (125 ml) freshly squeezed lime juice
2 teaspoons shaved palm sugar or dark brown sugar
2 teaspoons fish sauce
1 teaspoon finely chopped green onion
1 teaspoon finely chopped, deseeded red chili pepper
1 teaspoon grated fresh ginger

Place the lime juice in a bowl. Add the sugar and stir until it dissolves. Add all the other ingredients and mix well.

Makes $2/_3$ cup (150 ml)

Easy Plum Sauce

5 tablespoons plum jam
$1/_2$ cup (125 ml) rice wine vinegar
1 small red chili pepper, deseeded and thinly sliced

Place the jam and vinegar in a small saucepan and stir over medium heat until the jam melts, about 3 minutes. Remove from the heat and allow to cool. Just before serving, stir in the chili.

Makes 1 cup (250 ml)

Lime and Cilantro Dipping Sauce

2 tablespoons fish sauce
2 tablespoons white vinegar
2 tablespoons freshly squeezed lime juice
$1/_2$ teaspoon superfine (caster) sugar
2 tablespoons finely chopped cilantro (coriander leaves)

Combine all the ingredients in a small bowl and mix well.

Makes $1/_4$ cup (60 ml)

Chinese Barbecued Pork

2 pork fillets, 12 oz (350 g) each

Marinade
3 tablespoons hoisin sauce
3 tablespoons ground bean sauce
2 cloves garlic, crushed
$1/4$ teaspoon Chinese five spice powder
3 tablespoons soy sauce
Pinch of Chinese red food coloring powder (optional)
1 tablespoon brown sugar

1 Place the pork fillets in a shallow dish. In a small bowl, combine all the Marinade ingredients and mix well. Pour the Marinade over the pork and toss until well coated. Cover and refrigerate overnight.
2 Drain the marinated pork and reserve the Marinade. Place the marinated pork on a wire rack over a baking dish. Bake in a preheated oven at 350 °F (180 °C) for 30 minutes, basting with the Marinade and turning the pork during cooking. Remove from the oven and allow to stand for 10 minutes before slicing. Serve hot or cold.

Makes 8 small servings

Steamed Scallops with Ginger and Scallions

24 scallops in their shells
2 tablespoons oil
4 cloves garlic, minced
6 green onions, chopped

Ginger and Scallion Sauce
6 green onions, cut into shreds
1 tablespoon oil
2-in (5-cm) piece fresh ginger, cut into fine shreds
4 tablespoons soy sauce
2 tablespoons water

1 Clean the scallops and return to their shells. Heat the oil in a small saucepan over medium heat and stir-fry the garlic until aromatic, about 1 minute. Add the chopped green onion and stir-fry for 1 minute. Remove from the heat. Spoon the mixture over the scallops.
2 Half fill a medium wok with water (steamer should not touch water) and bring to a boil. Working in batches, arrange the scallops in a bamboo steamer, cover and place the steamer over the boiling water. Steam until the scallops are tender, 7 to 10 minutes. Lift the steamer off the wok and carefully remove the scallops.
3 To make the Ginger and Scallion Sauce, place the chopped green onion in a small bowl and set aside. Heat the oil in a small saucepan over medium heat and stir-fry the ginger until aromatic, about 1 minute. Add the soy sauce and water, and bring to a boil. Remove from the heat and pour the sauce over the green onion. Allow to stand for 2 minutes before serving with the scallops.

Makes 4 small servings

Steamed Clams with Blackbean Sauce

1 lb (500 g) fresh clams in shells, scrubbed clean

Blackbean Sauce
2 teaspoons oil
2 cloves garlic, minced
2 teaspoons grated fresh ginger
2 teaspoons fermented blackbeans (see note), rinsed
  and chopped
2 tablespoons soy sauce
$1/_3$ cup (90 ml) water
2 tablespoons oyster sauce

1 Place the clams in a bamboo steamer and cover. Half fill a medium wok with water (steamer should not touch water) and bring to a boil. Place the steamer over the boiling water and steam until the clam shells open, 3 to 4 minutes (discard any clams that do not open). Lift the steamer off the wok and carefully remove the clams.
2 To make the Blackbean Sauce, heat the oil in a small saucepan over medium heat. Stir-fry the garlic and ginger until aromatic, about 1 minute. Add the black beans and all the other ingredients, and bring to a boil. Reduce the heat to low and simmer uncovered for 1 minute. Remove from the heat and serve drizzled over the clams.

Note: Fermented black beans, also known as Chinese blackbeans, are small black soybeans that have been fermented and preserved in salt, hence their strong, salty flavor. These are not the same as blackbean sauce although blackbean sauce can be used as a substitute. Fermented blackbeans are sold in jars, packets or cans in Asian markets and can be kept for several months if stored in the refrigerator. Soak in warm water for 30 minutes before using, to remove excess salt.

Serves 4

Stir-fried Spicy Squid

4 cleaned medium squids (about 12 oz/350 g in total),
  tubes only, cleaned
1 tablespoon oil
1 teaspoon sesame oil
3 cloves garlic, minced
1 to 2 small red chili peppers, deseeded and minced

1 Cut each squid tube in half lengthwise, then cut into
strips $^3/_4$ in (2 cm) wide. Set aside.
2 Heat the oil in a wok or skillet over medium heat and
stir-fry the garlic and chili until aromatic, about 1
minute. Add the squid and stir-fry for 1 more minute.
Do not overcook or the squid will become tough.
Remove from the heat and serve hot.

Serves 2 to 4

Chinese Vegetables with Oyster Sauce

1 lb (500 g) garlic chives (see note),
  or other Chinese vegetable
  (Chinese broccoli (kailan) or
  choy sum or bok choy), trimmed
  into 4-in (10-cm) lengths and
  tied with string

Sauce
2 tablespoons oyster sauce
3 tablespoons chicken stock
2 teaspoons soy sauce
1 teaspoon sesame oil
1 teaspoon cornstarch, mixed
  with 1 tablespoon chicken stock

Serves 4

1 Make the Sauce by combining all the ingredients
except the cornstarch mixture in a small saucepan.
Bring to a boil over medium heat and add the cornstarch
mixture, stirring until the Sauce bubbles and thickens.
Remove from the heat.
2 Blanch the garlic chives in a saucepan of boiling
water for about 1 minute. Remove from the pan and
place on a serving platter. Remove the string and tie
one of the chives around the bundle. Pour the Sauce
over the blanched chives and serve hot.

Note: Garlic chives, also known as Chinese chives, have a
garlicky flavor and aroma. Unlike Western chives which
have round stems, garlic chives resemble flat green
onions and are sold in bunches in the produce section of
Asian food stores. When buying, look for fresh stems—
the ends should snap off easily.

Grilled Chinese Mushrooms

13 oz (400 g) fresh shiitake mushrooms, stems
  trimmed and discarded
2 teaspoons black sesame seeds, mixed with 1 teaspoon
  chopped garlic chive

Marinade
2 tablespoons soy sauce
2 tablespoons mirin
1 tablespoon superfine (caster) sugar
1 tablespoon chopped garlic chives

1 Place the mushrooms in a shallow dish. Combine the
Marinade ingredients in a small bowl and mix well.
Pour the Marinade over the mushrooms and mix until
well coated, cover and marinate for 5 minutes. Drain
the mushrooms and reserve the Marinade.
2 Place the seasoned mushrooms on a lightly greased
tray and grill under a preheated broiler (grill) until
softened, about 3 minutes on each side. Brush with
the Marinade during cooking. Arrange the grilled
mushrooms in small bowls or plates, sprinkle with the
black sesame seed and chive mixture, and serve hot.

Serves 4

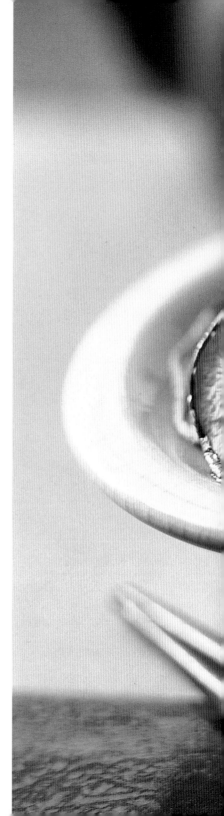

Steamed Pork Ribs

1 lb (500 g) pork spareribs, trimmed and separated
1 tablespoon rice wine
1 teaspoon salt
2 teaspoons superfine (caster) sugar
1 teaspoon sesame oil
4 cloves garlic, minced
2 tablespoons fermented blackbeans (page 22), chopped
$1/2$ teaspoon dry chili flakes
2 teaspoons cornstarch
$1/2$ red bell pepper, deseeded and finely shredded, to garnish

1 Place the ribs in a shallow dish. Combine the rice wine, salt, sugar, sesame oil, garlic, blackbeans, chili flakes and cornstarch, and mix well. Pour over the ribs, mix until well coated, cover and refrigerate for 2 hours. Transfer to a heatproof dish.
2 Half fill a medium wok with water (steamer should not touch water) and bring to a boil. Working in batches, place the ribs in a bamboo steamer. Cover and place the steamer over the boiling water. Steam until the ribs are tender, about 25 minutes. Lift the steamer off the wok and carefully remove the ribs. Serve hot, garnished with shredded red bell pepper.

Makes 8 small servings

Siew Mai Dumplings

32 wonton wrappers
Soy sauce or Ginger Soy Dipping
  Sauce (page 16), for dipping

Siew Mai Filling
6 Chinese dried mushrooms
4 oz (125 g) jumbo shrimp (or
  tiger prawns), peeled, deveined
  and finely chopped
8 oz (250 g) ground pork
4 green onions, finely chopped
$1/_2$ teaspoon salt
1 teaspoon sugar
1 tablespoon oyster sauce
1 teaspoon sesame oil
1 tablespoon cornstarch

Makes 32 dumplings

1 To make the Siew Mai Filling, in a small bowl, soak the mushrooms in boiling water until softened. Drain and squeeze out extra liquid from the mushrooms. Remove and discard the thick stems, finely chop the caps. Combine the chopped mushroom with all the other ingredients and mix until well blended.

2 Place the wonton wrappers on a work surface and cover with a damp kitchen towel. Working with one wrapper at a time, lay it on the work surface and spoon 1 tablespoon of the Siew Mai Filling to the center. Gather the edges of the wrapper around the filling, forming a basket, and gently squeeze the center of the dumpling to expose the filling at the top. Lightly tap the bottom of the dumpling on the work surface to flatten, cover with a damp kitchen towel and set aside. Continue to make the dumplings in the same manner with the remaining ingredients.

3 Line a medium bamboo steamer with parchment (baking paper). Half fill a medium wok with water (steamer should not touch water) and bring to a boil. Arrange the dumplings in a steamer, cover and place the steamer over the boiling water. Steam for 10 minutes. Lift the steamer off the wok and carefully remove the dumplings. Serve warm with dipping bowls of soy sauce or Ginger Soy Dipping Sauce (page 16).

Steamed Shanghai Dumplings (Xiao Long Bao)

Sometimes known as Shanghai street dumplings and originally made in the 1950s on the streets of Hong Kong on coal stoves by Shanghai refugees, these dumplings are still a favorite.

32 wonton wrappers
4 tablespoons oil
$^2/_3$ cup (150 ml) water
Soy sauce or Easy Plum Sauce
  (page 17), for dipping

Pork Filling
8 oz (250 g) bok choy
8 oz (250 g) ground pork
1 tablespoon grated fresh ginger
$^1/_2$ teaspoon salt
$^1/_2$ teaspoon sesame oil
$^1/_2$ teaspoon white vinegar
1 tablespoon oyster sauce

1 Prepare the Pork Filling by blanching the bok choy in a saucepan of boiling water for 2 minutes, then draining and refreshing in cold water. Finely chop the bok choy. In a bowl, combine the bok choy with all the other ingredients. Using wet hands, mix until well blended.
2 To shape the dumplings, place the wonton wrappers on a work surface and cover with a damp kitchen towel. Working with one wrapper at a time, lay it on the work surface and place 1 tablespoon of the Pork Filling in the center. Brush the edges of the wrapper with a little water, then gather the edges together and twist to seal. Place the dumpling on a plate, sealed side down, cover with a damp kitchen towel and set aside. Continue to make the dumplings in the same manner with the remaining ingredients.
3 Heat 2 tablespoons of the oil in a wok or skillet over medium heat. Working in 2 batches, fry the first batch of dumplings, sealed side down, until golden, about 3 minutes. Carefully add $^1/_2$ of the water (the liquid will sizzle and spatter a little; so be careful) and cook until the water evaporates. Reduce the heat to low and continue to cook until the dumplings are translucent, 3 to 4 minutes. Remove from the pan. Repeat with the remaining dumplings. Serve the dumplings warm with dipping bowls of soy sauce or Easy Plum Sauce (page 17).

Makes 32 dumplings

Flower Dumplings

40 wonton wrappers

Soy sauce or Ginger Soy Dipping Sauce (page 16), for dipping

Chicken Filling

1 lb (500 g) ground chicken

6 canned water chestnuts, drained and finely chopped

1 small carrot, peeled and finely chopped

2 green onions, finely chopped

1 teaspoon grated fresh ginger

1 teaspoon sesame oil

1 teaspoon rice wine

1 teaspoon soy sauce

1 teaspoon salt

2 teaspoons sugar

1 tablespoon oyster sauce

2 tablespoons cornstarch

1 Prepare the Chicken Filling by combining all the ingredients in a mixing bowl. Using wet hands, mix until well blended.

2 To make the dumplings, place the wonton wrappers on a work surface and cover with a damp kitchen towel. Working with one wrapper at a time, lay it on the work surface and place 1 tablespoon of the Chicken Filling in the center. Gather the edges of the wrapper around the filling, forming a basket, and gently squeeze the center of the dumpling to expose the filling at the top. Lightly tap the bottom of the dumpling on the work surface to flatten, cover with a damp kitchen towel and set aside. Continue to make the dumplings in the same manner with the remaining ingredients.

3 Line a medium bamboo steamer with parchment (baking paper). Half fill a medium wok with water (steamer should not touch water) and bring to a boil. Arrange the dumplings in a steamer, cover and place the steamer over the boiling water. Steam for 12 minutes. Lift the steamer off the wok and carefully remove the dumplings. Serve warm with dipping bowls of soy sauce or Ginger Soy Dipping Sauce (page 16).

Makes 40 dumplings

Salmon Dumplings with Cream Cheese

This recipe is a tasty Western adaptation of a traditional favorite.

24 wonton wrappers
24 garlic chives (page 26)
Soy sauce or bottled Thai sweet
   chili sauce (see note), for dipping

Filling
8 oz (250 g) salmon, bones and
   skin removed, finely chopped
3 tablespoons cream cheese
3 green onions, finely chopped
2 teaspoons grated fresh ginger
$1/_4$ teaspoon salt
Pinch of Chinese five spice
   powder
1 teaspoon grated lime rind
1 egg yolk

Makes 24 dumplings

1 Prepare the Filling by combining all the ingredients in a bowl. Using wet hands, mix until well blended.
2 To make the dumplings, place the wonton wrappers on a work surface and cover with a damp kitchen towel. Working with one wrapper at a time, lay it on the work surface and place 2 teaspoons of the Filling in the center. Brush the edges of the wrapper with a little water, then gather the edges together and twist to seal. Cover with a damp kitchen towel and set aside. Continue to make the dumplings in the same manner with the remaining ingredients.
3 Line a medium bamboo steamer with parchment (baking paper). Half fill a medium wok with water (steamer should not touch water) and bring to a boil. Arrange the dumplings in a steamer, cover and place the steamer over the boiling water. Steam for 8 minutes. Lift the steamer off the wok and carefully remove the dumplings. Transfer to serving platters.
4 Dip the chives into a bowl of hot water and tie one loosely around the top of each money bag. Serve warm with dipping bowls of soy sauce or Thai sweet chili sauce.

Note: Bamboo steamers may be stacked on top of one another to cook several different dishes at the same time, or to cook the same dish in batches. Thai chili sauce is used mainly as a dipping sauce. The sweet version is known as Thai sweet chili sauce and it goes particular well with either chicken or seafood, and is so labeled. Available in bottles or jars in Asian food stores.

Steamed Chicken Dumplings

These dumplings are so named because they resemble the crest of a rooster.

16 round wonton wrappers
6 cups (1¹/₂ liters) water
1 tablespoon oil
1 teaspoon salt
Lime and Cilantro Dipping Sauce
  (page 17), for dipping

Filling
8 oz (250 g) ground chicken
4 green onions, finely chopped
1 teaspoon grated fresh ginger
3 canned water chestnuts,
  drained and finely chopped
2 tablespoons finely chopped,
  drained canned bamboo shoots
1 teaspoon rice wine
1 teaspoon salt
1 teaspoon sugar
1 teaspoon soy sauce
1 teaspoon sesame oil
1 tablespoon oyster sauce
1¹/₂ tablespoons cornstarch

Makes 16 dumplings

1 Prepare the Filling by combining all the ingredients in a bowl. Using wet hands, mix until well blended.

2 Prepare the Lime and Cilantro Dipping Sauce following the recipe on page 17. Set aside.

3 To make the dumplings, place the wonton wrappers on a work surface and cover with a damp kitchen towel. Working with one wrapper at a time, place it in a dumpling press and spoon 1¹/₂ tablespoons of the Filling to the center. Brush the edges of the wrapper with a little water, then close the press firmly to seal the edges together. Alternatively, place the wrapper on the work surface, spoon in the Filling, wet the edges and fold the wrapper in half to form a semicircle. Pinch the edges together to make a frill. Cover with a damp kitchen towel and set aside. Continue to make the dumplings in the same manner with the remaining ingredients.

4 Pour the water into a medium wok or saucepan, add the oil and salt, and bring to a boil. Working in batches, drop the dumplings into the boiling water to cook for 3 to 5 minutes. Remove the cooked dumplings from the pan with a slotted spoon and run cold water over them. Serve immediately with the Lime and Cilantro Dipping Sauce (page 17).

Steamed Spinach Dumplings

24 wonton wrappers
Soy sauce, for dipping

Spinach Filling
1 tablespoon oil
1 tablespoon grated fresh ginger
3 cloves garlic, crushed
10 oz (300 g) spinach, washed and finely chopped
$1/_2$ teaspoon salt

1 Make the Spinach Filling by heating the oil in a wok or skillet over medium heat. Add the ginger and garlic, and stir-fry until aromatic, about 1 minute. Add the spinach and stir-fry until soft, 2 to 3 minutes. Remove from the heat and season with the salt. Transfer the Spinach Filling to a bowl and allow to cool completely.
2 To make the dumplings, place the wonton wrappers on a work surface and cover with a damp kitchen towel. Working with one wrapper at a time, lay it on the work surface and place 2 teaspoons of the Spinach Filling in the center. Brush the edges of the wrapper with a little water, then gather the edges together and twist to seal. Cover with a damp kitchen towel and set aside. Continue to make the dumplings in the same manner with the remaining ingredients.
3 Line a medium bamboo steamer with parchment (baking paper). Half fill a medium wok with water (steamer should not touch water) and bring to a boil. Arrange the dumplings in a steamer, cover and place the steamer over the boiling water. Steam for 10 minutes. Lift the steamer off the wok and carefully remove the dumplings. Serve warm with dipping bowls of soy sauce.

Makes 24 dumplings

Snowpea Shoot Dumplings

16 round wonton wrappers
Soy sauce, for dipping

Filling
4 oz (125 g) fresh snowpea
  shoots, coarsely chopped
4 oz (125 g) jumbo shrimp (or
  tiger prawns), peeled, deveined
  and coarsely chopped
2 teaspoons grated fresh ginger
3 teaspoons oyster sauce
1 teaspoon soy sauce
1 teaspoon rice wine
$1/_4$ teaspoon salt
$1/_2$ teaspoon sugar
1 teaspoon sesame oil
1 tablespoon cornstarch

Makes 16 dumplings

1 Make the Filling by blanching the snowpea shoots in a saucepan of boiling water for 1 minute. Remove from the heat, drain and refresh immediately in cold water. Combine all the ingredients in a bowl. Using wet hands, mix until well blended.

2 To make the dumplings, place the wonton wrappers on a work surface and cover with a damp kitchen towel. Working with one wrapper at a time, lay it on the work surface and place 1 tablespoon of the Filling in the center. Brush the edges of the wrapper with a little water, and fold three sides of the wrapper into the center, forming a triangular shape. Using your fingertips, press the edges of the wrapper together. Cover with a damp kitchen towel and set aside. Continue to make the dumplings in the same manner with the remaining ingredients.

3 Line a medium bamboo steamer with parchment (baking paper). Half fill a medium wok with water (steamer should not touch water) and bring to a boil. Arrange the dumplings in a steamer, cover and place the steamer over the boiling water. Steam for 10 minutes. Lift the steamer off the wok and carefully remove the dumplings. Serve warm with dipping bowls of soy sauce.

Steamed Barbecued Pork Buns (Char Siew Bao)

Soy sauce and hoisin sauce, for
dipping

Dough
$1^1/_2$ teaspoons active dry yeast
$^1/_2$ cup (125 ml) warm water
4 tablespoons superfine (caster)
sugar
1 cup (150 g) flour
$^1/_2$ cup (60 g) self-rising flour
3 teaspoons butter, melted

Filling
1 tablespoon oil
3 teaspoons grated fresh ginger
2 cloves garlic, chopped
1 tablespoon hoisin sauce
1 tablespoon oyster sauce
1 tablespoon soy sauce
1 teaspoon sesame oil
3 teaspoons cornstarch, mixed
with 1 tablespoon water
8 oz (250 g) Chinese barbecue
pork, finely chopped
6 green onions, finely chopped

Makes 16 buns

1 Make the Dough by combining the yeast with
2 tablespoons of the warm water, 1 teaspoon of the
sugar and 1 teaspoon of the flour in a small bowl. Mix
until well blended. Cover with a kitchen towel and
allow to stand in a warm place until frothy, about
15 minutes. Sift the remaining flour and self-rising
flour into a large bowl. Add the remaining water and
sugar, yeast mixture and the melted butter. Using a
wooden spoon, mix the mixture into a soft Dough.
Turn out onto a floured work surface and knead until
smooth and elastic, 3 to 5 minutes. Place the Dough in
a large greased bowl, cover and allow to stand in a
warm place until doubled in size, about 1 hour.
2 To make the Filling, heat the oil in a wok or skillet
over medium heat and stir-fry the ginger and garlic until
aromatic, about 1 minute. Add the hoisin sauce, oyster
sauce, soy sauce and sesame oil. Cook, stirring, for 2
minutes. Add the cornstarch mixture, bring to a boil and
stir until the sauce thickens, about 2 minutes. Remove
from the heat and stir in the pork and chopped green
onion. Transfer to a bowl and allow to cool completely.
3 Punch down the Dough. Turn out onto a floured
work surface and knead until smooth, about 5 minutes.
Divide the Dough into 16 equal pieces and roll or
press out each piece to form a $2^1/_2$-in (6-cm) circle.
Cover the dough circles with a damp kitchen towel.
Working with one dough circle at a time, spoon $1^1/_2$
tablespoons of the Filling onto the center. Gather the
edges of the dough circle together and twist to seal
into a bun. Cover the bun with a kitchen towel.
Continue to make the buns in the same manner with
the remaining ingredients.
4 Cut out 16 squares of parchment (baking paper) and
place the buns, sealed side down, on the paper. Half
fill a medium wok with water (steamer should not
touch water) and bring to a boil. Working in batches,
arrange the buns in a steamer, cover and place the
steamer over the boiling water. Steam for 15 minutes.
Serve the buns warm with serving bowls of soy sauce
and hoisin sauce on the side.

Steamed Chicken Buns

Sweet Cilantro Dip (page 16), for dipping

Dough
2$^1/_2$ cups (375 g) flour
3 teaspoons baking powder
$^1/_2$ cup (110 g) superfine (caster) sugar
$^1/_2$ cup (125 ml) milk
$^1/_3$ cup (90 ml) water
$^1/_4$ cup (60 ml) oil

Filling
6 Chinese dried mushrooms
1 tablespoon oil
3 teaspoons grated fresh ginger
8 oz (250 g) ground chicken
2 tablespoons chopped, drained canned bamboo shoots
4 green onions, chopped
1 tablespoon oyster sauce
1 teaspoon soy sauce
1 teaspoon sesame oil
$^1/_4$ teaspoon salt
2 teaspoons cornstarch, mixed with 2 tablespoons chicken stock

1 Prepare the Dough by sifting the flour and baking powder into a bowl. Add the sugar, and gradually add the combined milk, water and oil, mixing to form a soft Dough. Turn out onto a floured work surface and knead until smooth, 1 to 2 minutes. Wrap the Dough in plastic wrap and chill in the refrigerator for 1 hour.
2 Prepare the Sweet Cilantro Dip following the recipe on page 16. Set aside.
3 To make the Filling, soak the mushrooms in a small bowl of boiling water until softened, 15 to 30 minutes, then drain and squeeze out the excess liquid from the mushrooms. Remove and discard the thick stems, and finely chop the caps. Heat the oil in a wok or skillet over medium heat and stir-fry the ginger until aromatic, about 1 minute. Add the ground chicken and stir-fry until it changes color, about 3 minutes. Stir in the chopped bamboo shoot and green onion, and seasoned with the oyster sauce, soy sauce, sesame oil and salt. Add the cornstarch mixture and bring the ingredients to a boil, stirring until the sauce thickens. Remove from the heat, transfer to a plate and allow to cool completely.
4 Roll the Dough into a sausage shape 16 in (40$^1/_2$ cm) long. Slice into sixteen 1-in (2$^1/_2$-cm) pieces and roll each into a ball. Cover with a damp kitchen towel. Working with a piece of the Dough at a time, press into a cup shape. Place 1$^1/_2$ tablespoons of the Filling in the center of the dough cup. Gather the edges together, twist and seal into a bun. Cover with a damp kitchen towel and continue to make the buns in the same manner with the remaining ingredients.
5 Cut out 16 squares of parchment (baking paper) and place the buns, sealed side down, on the paper. Half fill a medium wok with water (steamer should not touch water) and bring to a boil. Working in batches, arrange the buns in a steamer, cover and place the steamer over the boiling water. Steam for 20 minutes. Serve the buns with dipping bowls of the Sweet Cilantro Dip (page 16).

Makes 16 buns

Steamed Vegetable Buns

Soy sauce, or Sweet Cilantro Dip (page 16) or Chili Sauce (page 16), for dipping

Dough
1 1/2 teaspoons active dry yeast
1/2 cup (125 ml) warm water
4 tablespoons superfine (caster) sugar
1 cup (150 g) flour
1/2 cup (60 g) self-rising flour
3 teaspoons butter, melted

Filling
1 tablespoon oil
1 teaspoon grated fresh ginger
2 cloves garlic, chopped
5 oz (150 g) bok choy, finely chopped
4 oz (125 g) choy sum, finely chopped
1 carrot, peeled, finely chopped
6 green onions, finely chopped
1 teaspoon sesame oil
2 tablespoons bottled Thai sweet chili sauce (page 38)

1 Make the Dough by combining the yeast with 2 tablespoons of the warm water, 1 teaspoon of the sugar and 1 teaspoon of the flour in a small bowl. Mix until well blended. Cover with a kitchen towel and allow to stand in a warm place until frothy, about 15 minutes. Sift the remaining flour and self-rising flour into a large bowl. Add the remaining water and sugar, yeast mixture and the melted butter. Using a wooden spoon, mix the mixture into a soft Dough. Turn out onto a floured work surface and knead until smooth and elastic, 3 to 5 minutes. Place the Dough in a large greased bowl, cover and allow to stand in a warm place until doubled in size, about 1 hour.

2 To make the Filling, heat the oil in a wok or skillet over medium heat and stir-fry the ginger and garlic until aromatic, about 1 minute. Add the vegetables and stir-fry for 2 minutes. Remove from the heat and stir in the sesame oil and chili sauce. Transfer to a bowl and allow to cool completely.

3 Punch down the Dough. Turn out onto a floured work surface and knead until smooth, about 5 minutes. Divide the Dough into 16 equal pieces and roll or press out each piece to form a 2 1/2-in (6-cm) circle. Cover the dough circles with a damp kitchen towel. Working with one dough circle at a time, spoon 1 1/2 tablespoons of the Filling onto the center. Gather the edges of the dough circle together and twist to seal into a bun. Cover with a kitchen towel. Continue to make the buns in the same manner with the remaining ingredients.

4 Cut out 16 squares of parchment (baking paper) and place the buns, sealed side down, on the paper. Half fill a medium wok with water (steamer should not touch water) and bring to a boil. Working in batches, arrange the buns in a steamer, cover and place the steamer over the boiling water. Steam for 15 minutes. Serve the buns warm with dipping bowls of soy sauce or Sweet Cilantro Sauce, or Chili Sauce (page 16).

Makes 16 buns

Chinese Pork Sausage Buns

1 cup (125 g) self-rising flour
2 teaspoons baking powder
2 teaspoons superfine (caster) sugar
2 teaspoons lard
$1/4$ –$1/3$ cup (60–90 ml) warm milk
6 sweet dried Chinese pork sausages (*lap cheong*)
2 teaspoons soy sauce
1 tablespoon hoisin sauce, plus extra for dipping

Makes 12 buns

1 Sift the flour and baking powder into a bowl and add the sugar. Rub the lard into the dry ingredients using your fingertips. Gradually add enough milk to make a soft dough. Turn the dough out onto a floured work surface and knead for 1 to 2 minutes, until smooth. Wrap the dough in plastic wrap and allow to stand for 30 minutes.

2 Meanwhile, cut the sausages in half crosswise. Place in a bowl with the soy sauce and 1 tablespoon of the hoisin sauce, and mix until well coated. Cover and allow to stand for 25 minutes.

3 Turn the dough out onto a floured work surface and knead for 1 minute. Roll into a thick cylinder 12 in (30 cm) long, and slice it into 12 equal pieces. Cover the dough pieces with a damp kitchen towel to prevent drying out. Working with one piece of the dough at a time, rub it between the floured hands to form a thin cylinder about 4 in (10 cm) long. Wrap the dough around a sausage half in a spiral pattern, leaving the ends of the sausage exposed, and place on a greased tray. Continue to make the sausage buns in the same manner with the remaining ingredients.

4 Line a bamboo steamer with banana leaves or parchment (baking paper). Half fill a medium wok with water (steamer should not touch water) and bring to a boil. Working in batches, arrange the buns in the prepared steamer, allowing room for the buns to spread. Cover and place the steamer over the boiling water and steam for 15 minutes. Serve the buns warm with dipping bowls of hoisin sauce.

Spring Rolls

24 frozen mini spring roll wrappers, each $4^1/_2$-in (12-cm) square, thawed
2 teaspoons cornstarch, mixed with 2 tablespoons water
Oil, for deep-frying
Quick Sweet and Sour Sauce (page 17), for dipping

Filling
2 tablespoons oil
2 cloves garlic, minced
2 teaspoons grated fresh ginger
3 oz (100 g) ground pork
3 oz (100 g) ground chicken
2 oz (60 g) ground shrimp (prawns)
2 stalks celery, finely chopped
1 small carrot, peeled and finely chopped
6 canned water chestnuts, drained and finely chopped
4 green onions, finely chopped
1 cup (90 g) shredded Chinese or Napa cabbage
2 teaspoons cornstarch
2 tablespoons oyster sauce
1 tablespoon soy sauce
2 tablespoons chicken stock
1 teaspoon sesame oil

Makes 24 spring rolls

1 Prepare the Filling by heating 1 tablespoon of the oil in a wok or skillet over medium heat. Stir-fry the garlic and ginger until aromatic, about 1 minute. Add the ground pork, chicken and shrimp, and stir-fry until the mixture changes color, about 3 minutes. Remove from the heat and transfer to a bowl. Set aside.
2 Using the same wok or skillet, heat the remaining oil over medium heat. Add the vegetables, increase the heat to high and stir-fry until softened, about 2 minutes. In a small bowl, combine the cornstarch, oyster sauce, soy sauce and chicken stock, and add to the wok or skillet. Bring the ingredients to a boil, reduce the heat to medium and simmer uncovered until the sauce thickens, 1 to 2 minutes. Remove from the heat and allow to cool completely. Stir in the cooled pork mixture and sesame oil, and mix well.
3 Prepare the Quick Sweet and Sour Sauce following the recipe on page 17. Set aside.
4 To make the spring rolls, separate the wrappers and cover with a damp kitchen towel. Working with a wrapper at a time, lay it on a work surface and, using your fingertips, wet the edges with the cornstarch mixture. Spoon 1 tablespoon of the Filling onto the center of the wrapper and roll up diagonally, tucking in the edges. Seal with the cornstarch mixture. Continue to make the spring rolls with the remaining ingredients.
5 Heat the oil in a large wok until it reaches 375°F (190°C) on a deep-frying thermometer, or until a small bread cube dropped in the hot oil sizzles and turns golden. Working in batches, deep-fry the spring rolls until golden, about 1 minute. Using a slotted spoon, remove from the hot oil and drain on paper towels. Serve the spring rolls with dipping bowls of the Quick Sweet and Sour Sauce (page 17) on the side.

Roast Duck Pancakes

4 tablespoons hoisin sauce
1 tablespoon rice wine
15 garlic chives (page 26), to fasten
Hoisin sauce, for dipping

Pancakes
2 eggs, beaten
$3/4$ cup (185 ml) water
4 tablespoons milk
2 teaspoons superfine (caster)
   sugar
$3/4$ cup (90 g) flour
$1/3$ cup (45 g) cornstarch
1 tablespoon oil

Filling
15 green onions
2 carrots, peeled and cut into thin
   matchsticks
1 Chinese roast duck

Makes about 15 rolls

1 Make the Pancakes by whisking together the eggs, water, milk and sugar in a bowl. Sift the flour and cornstarch into another bowl. Make a well in the center and gradually add in the egg mixture, beating to form a smooth batter.

2 Heat a little oil in a non-stick skillet over medium heat. Pour in 2 tablespoons of the batter and swirl the pan gently to form a thin round Pancake. Cook until golden, about 2 minutes. Turn and cook the other side for 10 seconds. Remove from the pan and continue to make the Pancakes with the remaining batter and oil.

3 Prepare the Filling by cutting into each end of the green onions with a sharp knife or scissors to form a fringe. Place the spring onions and carrots in a bowl of iced water and refrigerate for 15 minutes, or until the green onions curl. Remove the meat and skin from the roast duck and roughly chop.

4 Combine the rice wine and hoisin sauce in a bowl and mix well.

5 To make the pancake rolls, lay one Pancake on a work surface and place 1 tablespoon of the duck meat and skin in the center. Spread 1 teaspoon of the hoisin and rice wine mixture on top and add 1 green onion curl and 3 to 4 carrot sticks. Fold one end of the Pancake over the Filling, roll up tightly and secure with a chive, trimming off the excess. Continue to make the pancake rolls in the same manner with the remaining ingredients. Serve the pancake rolls immediately with dipping bowls of hoisin sauce.

Shrimp Pancake Rolls

2 eggs, beaten
3 tablespoons water
2 teaspoons cornstarch
4 tablespoons oil
Soy, or hoisin or plum sauce, for
  dipping

Pancakes
1$^1/_2$ cups (220 g) flour
2$^1/_2$ cups (625 ml) water
2 eggs, beaten
3 tablespoons oil

Filling
1 tablespoon oil
2 teaspoons grated fresh ginger
1 carrot, peeled and grated
1 stick celery, finely chopped
8 oz (250 g) jumbo shrimp (or
  tiger prawns), peeled, deveined
  and finely chopped
1 cup (50 g) bean sprouts
4 tablespoons finely chopped
  cucumber
1 tablespoon soy sauce
1 tablespoon rice wine
1 teaspoon sesame oil
2 teaspoons cornstarch

Makes about 25 rolls

1 Make the Pancake by sifting the flour into a medium bowl. Make a well in the center and whisk in the combined water and eggs, mixing to form a smooth batter. Heat 2 teaspoons of the oil in a non-stick skillet over medium heat. Add 2 tablespoons of the batter and swirl the pan gently to form a thin round Pancake. Cook until the batter bubbles and set, about 1 minute. Turn and cook the other side for 30 seconds. Remove the Pancake from the skillet and continue to make the Pancakes with the remaining batter and oil.
2 Prepare the Filling by heating the oil in a wok or skillet over medium heat and stir-frying the ginger until aromatic, about 1 minute. Add the carrot, celery and shrimp, and stir-fry until the shrimp changes color, about 2 minutes. Stir in the bean sprouts and cucumber. Combine the soy sauce, rice wine, sesame oil and cornstarch in a small bowl, mix well and add to the pan. Bring the mixture to a boil and simmer until thickens, 2 to 3 minutes. Remove from the heat, transfer the Filling to a plate and set aside to cool completely.
3 To make the pancake rolls, lay one Pancake on a work surface and place 1 tablespoon of the Filling in the center. Fold one end of the Pancake over the Filling, tuck in the sides and roll up tightly. Continue making the rolls in the same manner with the remaining ingredients.
4 Combine the eggs, water and cornstarch in a shallow dish. Heat the oil in a skillet over medium heat. Working with a few at a time, dip the pancake rolls into the egg mixture, allowing the excess to drain off, and pan-fry the rolls until golden on both sides, 2 to 3 minutes. Remove from the pan and serve hot with dipping bowls of soy, hoisin or plum sauce.

Paper-wrapped Shrimp Rolls

20 rice paper wrappers, each
8 in (20 cm) square, or spring
roll wrappers (page 55)
2 tablespoons cornstarch, mixed
with 1$^1/_2$ tablespoons water
4 tablespoons oil
Hoisin sauce, for dipping

Shrimp Filling
1$^1/_2$ lbs (750 g) jumbo shrimp (or
tiger prawns), peeled, deveined
and finely chopped
3 teaspoons grated fresh ginger
2 cloves garlic, minced
4 green onions, finely chopped
1 tablespoon cornstarch

Makes 20

1 Prepare the Shrimp Filling by combining the shrimp, ginger, garlic, chopped green onion and cornstarch in a bowl. Using wet hands, mix until well blended.
2 To make the shrimp rolls, working with a wrapper at a time, briefly dip it in a shallow bowl of warm water until softened. Remove and lay it on a work surface. Spoon 1$^1/_2$ tablespoons of the Shrimp Filling to the center and brush the edges of the wrapper with the cornstarch mixture. Fold one end of the wrapper over the Shrimp Filling, tucking in the sides, and roll up tightly to form a neat roll. Cover with a damp kitchen towel and set aside. Continue to make the shrimp rolls in the same manner with the remaining ingredients.
3 Heat the oil in a wok or skillet, until it reaches 375 °F (190 °C) on a deep-frying thermometer, or until a small bread cube dropped in the hot oil sizzles and turns golden. Working in batches, deep-fry the shrimp rolls until golden on both sides, about 2 minutes. Remove from the hot oil and drain on paper towels. Serve hot with dipping bowls of hoisin sauce on the side.

Vegetable Spring Rolls

24 frozen mini spring roll
  wrappers, each $4^1/_2$-in (12-cm)
  square, thawed
2 teaspoons cornstarch, mixed
  with 2 tablespoons water
Oil, for deep-frying
Easy Plum Sauce (page 17), for
  dipping

Vegetable Filling

1 tablespoon oil
2 cloves garlic, minced
2 teaspoons grated fresh ginger
6 green onions, finely chopped
2 stalks celery, finely chopped
2 cups (200 g) grated carrot
2 cups (250 g) shredded Chinese
  or napa cabbage
1 cup (50 g) bean sprouts, tails
  removed
3 tablespoons finely chopped,
  drained canned water chestnuts
$1/_2$ cup (20 g) finely chopped
  fried bean curd
3 teaspoons cornstarch, mixed
  with 1 tablespoon water
2 teaspoons sesame oil
2 teaspoons soy sauce

Makes 24 rolls

1 Prepare the Vegetable Filling by heating the oil in a wok over medium heat. Stir-fry the garlic and ginger until aromatic, about 1 minute. Stir in the chopped green onion, celery, carrot and cabbage, and cook until soften, about 3 minutes. Add the bean sprouts, chopped water chestnut and fried bean curd, cover and cook for 2 minutes. Pour in the cornstarch mixture, sesame oil and soy sauce and bring the mixture to a boil. Reduce the heat to low and simmer, stirring, until the sauce thickens, 1 to 2 minutes. Remove from the heat, transfer to a plate and allow to cool completely.
2 Make the Easy Plum Sauce as instructed on page 17.
3 To make the spring rolls, separate the wrappers and cover with a damp kitchen towel. Working with a wrapper at a time, lay it on a work surface and, using your fingertips, wet the edges with the cornstarch mixture. Spoon 2 tablespoons of the Vegetable Filling onto the center of the wrapper and roll up diagonally, tucking in the edges. Seal with the cornstarch mixture. Continue to make the spring rolls with the remaining ingredients.
4 Heat the oil in a large wok until it reaches 375 °F (190 °C) on a deep-frying thermometer, or until a small bread cube dropped in the oil sizzles and turns golden. Working in batches, deep-fry the spring rolls until golden, about 1 minute. Using a slotted spoon, remove the spring rolls from the oil and drain on paper towels. Serve hot with the Easy Plum Sauce (page 17).

Crispy Pork Wontons

24 square wonton wrappers
Oil, for deep-frying
Soy sauce or Lime Cilantro
  Dipping Sauce (page 17), for
  dipping

Filling
8 oz (250 g) ground pork
4 oz (125 g) jumbo shrimp (or
  tiger prawns), peeled, deveined
  and finely chopped
1 tablespoon grated fresh ginger
4 green onions, finely chopped
2 teaspoons rice wine
$1/_2$ teaspoon salt
1 teaspoon sesame oil
3 teaspoons cornstarch

Makes 24 wontons

1 Make the Filling by combining all the ingredients in a mixing bowl. Using wet hands, mix until well blended.
2 To make the wontons, place the wonton wrappers on a work surface and cover with a damp kitchen towel. Working with one wrapper at a time, lay it on the work surface and place 1 tablespoon of the Filling in the center. Brush the edges of the wrapper with a little water and fold the wrapper corners to the center, forming an envelope shape. Using your fingertips, press along diagonal edges to seal. Cover the wonton with a damp kitchen towel and continue making the wontons in the same manner with the remaining ingredients.
3 Heat the oil in a large wok until it reaches 375 °F (190 °C) on a deep-frying thermometer, or until a small bread cube dropped in the oil sizzles and turns golden. Working in batches, deep-fry the wontons until golden on both sides, 2 to 3 minutes. Remove from the oil with a slotted spoon and drain on paper towels. Serve hot with dipping bowls of soy sauce or Lime and Cilantro Dipping Sauce (page 17).

Crispy Wonton-wrapped Shrimp

20 jumbo shrimp (or tiger prawns),
  peeled and deveined, tails intact
2 cloves garlic, minced
2 tablespoons oil
20 wonton wrappers
1 egg, beaten
20 garlic chives (page 26)
Oil, for deep-frying
Soy sauce, or hoisin sauce or
  plum sauce, for dipping

1 Combine the shrimp, garlic and oil in a bowl and toss until well coated. Cover and refrigerate for 2 hours.

2 Dip the chives into a bowl of hot water for 1 minute and drain.

3 Place the wonton wrappers on a work surface and cover with a damp kitchen towel. Working with one wrapper at a time, brush the edges of the wrapper with the beaten egg. Place a shrimp diagonally across the center, fold the wrapper around the shrimp and secure with a chive, trimming off the excess. Cover with a damp kitchen towel and set aside. Continue to make the wontons in the same manner with the remaining ingredients.

4 Heat the oil in a large wok until it reaches 375 °F (190 °C) on a deep-frying thermometer, or until a small bread cube dropped in the oil sizzles and turns golden. Working in batches, deep-fry the wrapped shrimp until golden, 1 to 2 minutes. Remove from the hot oil using a slotted spoon and drain on paper towels. Serve hot with dipping bowls of soy, hoisin or plum sauce.

Makes 20 pieces

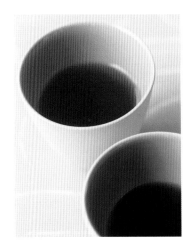

Golden Shrimp Balls

12 slices dry white bread
1 lb (500 g) jumbo shrimp (or
  tiger prawns), peeled and
  deveined
6 canned water chestnuts,
  drained and finely chopped
2 strips bacon, rind removed and
  minced
1 teaspoon sugar
$^1/_2$ teaspoon salt
2 teaspoons cornstarch
Oil, for deep-frying
Quick Sweet and Sour Sauce
  (page 17), for dipping

Makes 16 balls

1 Remove the crusts from the bread. Cut the bread into $^1/_4$-in (6-mm) cubes. Spread out the bread cubes on a tray and allow to dry at room temperature.
2 Flatten the shrimp with the back of a cleaver, then finely chop. Combine the shrimp, water chestnuts and bacon in a bowl and stir in the sugar, salt and cornstarch. Mix until well blended, cover and chill in the refrigerator for 30 minutes.
3 Prepare the Quick Sweet and Sour Sauce following the recipe on page 17. Set aside.
4 Wet your hands, spoon 3 tablespoons of the shrimp mixture and roll it into a ball. Roll the shrimp ball in the bread cubes to coat. Repeat with the remaining mixture to make a total of 16 balls.
5 Heat the oil in a large wok or saucepan until it reaches 375 °F (190 °C) on a deep-frying thermometer, or until a small bread cube dropped in the oil sizzles and turns golden. Working in batches, deep-fry the coated shrimp balls until golden, 1 to 2 minutes. Remove from the hot oil with a slotted spoon and drain on paper towels. Serve hot with dipping bowls of the Quick Sweet and Sour Sauce (page 17).

Crispy Chicken Money Bags

Money bags are shaped into little pouches gathered at the top,
reminiscent of the little leather sacs used to carry money in China.

24 wonton wrappers
Oil, for deep-frying
Soy sauce, or hoisin sauce or
  plum sauce, for dipping

Filling
3 oz (100 g) bok choy, washed
  and leaves separated
8 oz (250 g) ground chicken
1 teaspoon sesame oil
3 green onions, finely chopped
1 teaspoon grated fresh ginger
1 clove garlic, minced
1 teaspoon rice wine
2 teaspoons oyster sauce
1 teaspoon soy sauce
Pinch of salt, or to taste
3 teaspoons cornstarch

Makes 24 wontons

1 Prepare the Filling by blanching the bok choy in a saucepan of boiling water for 2 minutes. Remove from the heat, drain and refresh in cold water, then chop finely. In a bowl, combine the chopped bok choy with all the other ingredients. Using wet hands, mix until well combined.

2 To make the wontons, place the wonton wrappers on a work surface and cover with a damp kitchen towel. Working with one wrapper at a time, lay it on the work surface and place 1 tablespoon of the Filling in the center. Brush the edges of the wrapper with a little water, then gather the edges together and twist to seal. Cover with a damp kitchen towel and set aside. Continue to make the wontons in the same manner with the remaining ingredients.

3 Heat the oil in a large wok until it reaches 375 °F (190 °C) on a deep-frying thermometer, or until a small bread cube dropped in the oil sizzles and turns golden. Working in batches, deep-fry the wontons until golden, 1 to 2 minutes. Using a slotted spoon, remove the wontons from the hot oil and drain on paper towels. Serve hot with dipping bowls of soy, hoisin or plum sauce.

Crispy Shrimp Wontons

25 round wonton wrappers

Oil, for deep-frying

Soy sauce or Chili Sauce (page 16), for dipping

Filling

6 Chinese dried mushrooms

4 oz (125 g) jumbo shrimp (or tiger prawns), peeled, deveined and finely chopped

8 oz (250 g) ground pork

$1/_2$ cup (125 g) finely chopped, drained canned bamboo shoots

6 green onions, finely chopped

1 clove garlic, minced

2 teaspoons sesame oil

3 teaspoons soy sauce

2 teaspoons rice wine

Makes 25 wontons

1 Prepare the Filling by soaking the mushrooms in a small bowl of boiling water until softened, 15 to 30 minutes. Drain and squeeze the excess liquid from the mushrooms. Remove and discard the thick stems, finely chop the caps. Combine the chopped mushrooms with all the other ingredients in a bowl. Using wet hands, mix until well blended.

2 To make the wontons, place the wonton wrappers on a work surface and cover with a damp kitchen towel. Working with one wrapper at a time, place it in a dumpling press and spoon $1^1/_2$ tablespoons of the Filling to the center. Brush the edges of the wrapper with a little water, then close the press firmly to seal the edges together. Alternatively, place the wrapper on the work surface, spoon in the Filling, wet the edges and fold the wrapper in half to form a semicircle. Pinch the edges together to make a frill. Cover with a damp kitchen towel and set aside. Continue to make the wontons in the same manner with the remaining ingredients.

3 Heat the oil in a large wok until it reaches 375 °F (190 °C). Working in batches, deep-fry the wontons on both sides, 1 to 2 minutes. Using a slotted spoon, remove the wontons from the oil and drain on paper towels. Serve hot with dipping bowls of soy sauce or Chili Sauce (page 16).

Stuffed Crab Claws

12 cooked crab claws
1 lb (500 g) jumbo shrimp (or tiger prawns), peeled and deveined
2 cloves garlic
3 teaspoons grated fresh ginger
1 egg white
2 teaspoons fish sauce
$^1/_4$ teaspoon salt
4 green onions, coarsely chopped
4 tablespoons finely chopped celery
4 tablespoons cornstarch
Oil, for deep-frying
Chili Sauce (page 16) or Lime and Fish Sauce (page 17), for dipping

Batter
$^1/_2$ cup (60 g) cornstarch
$^1/_2$ cup (75 g) flour
$^1/_2$ teaspoon baking powder
$^1/_2$ teaspoon salt
1 cup (250 ml) water

Makes 12

1 The shell around the larger end of the crab claw is generally lightly cracked when purchased. Gently remove the shell, leaving the shell on the nipper end to make a handle for holding the crab claws. Place the shrimp, garlic, ginger, egg white, fish sauce and salt in a food processor and process until smooth. Transfer to a bowl and stir in the chopped green onion and celery. Divide the shrimp mixture into 12 portions. With wet hands, flatten each portion in the palm of your hand and place the flesh end of the crab claw into center of the shrimp mixture, wrapping the shrimp mixture around the crab flesh. Wet your hands again and mold the shrimp mixture evenly all over the crab flesh.
2 To make the Batter, sift the cornstarch, flour, baking powder and salt into a mixing bowl. Gradually add the water, mixing to a smooth Batter.
3 Heat the oil in a large wok or saucepan until it reaches 375 °F (190 °C). Dip the crab claws in the cornstarch and shake off any excess. Working in batches and holding the nipper end of the claws, dip the stuffed claws into the Batter, then drop into the hot oil. Deep-fry until golden, 2 to 3 minutes. Using a slotted spoon, remove from the oil and drain on paper towels. Serve hot with dipping bowls of the Chili Sauce (page 16) or Lime and Fish Sauce (page 17).

Shrimp Toasts

This Western-adapted recipe is a favorite in most dim sum tea houses.

4 slices dry white bread
1 egg, beaten
1 cup (60 g) breadcrumbs
Oil, for deep-frying
Sweet Cilantro Dip (page 16), or
    Quick Sweet and Sour Sauce
    (page 17)

Shrimp Filling
1 lb (500g) jumbo shrimp (or tiger
    prawns), peeled and deveined
2 cloves garlic
2 teaspoons grated fresh ginger
1 teaspoon sugar
$^1/_2$ teaspoon salt
1 tablespoon cornstarch
1 egg white
1 teaspoon sesame oil
4 green onions, finely chopped

Serves 4

1 Remove the crust from the bread and cut each slice diagonally into 4 triangles. Allow the bread to dry out at room temperature, or place in the oven on very low for about 30 minutes to allow it to dry out.

2 Make the Sweet Cilantro Dip or Quick Sweet and Sour Sauce following the recipe on page 16 or 17. Set aside.

3 To make the Shrimp Filling, process all the ingredients except the chopped green onion in a food processor until smooth. Transfer to a bowl and stir in the chopped green onion.

4 Spread 2 tablespoons of the Shrimp Filling in the center of each bread triangle. Brush the Shrimp Filling and bread edges with the beaten egg and sprinkle with breadcrumbs. Pat the topping into a pyramid shape, shaking off any excess crumbs.

5 Heat the oil in a large wok until it reaches 375 °F (190 °C) on a deep-frying thermometer, or until a small bread cube dropped in the hot oil sizzles and turns golden. Working in batches, deep-fry the coated bread triangles until golden on both sides, 1 to 2 minutes. Using a slotted spoon, remove the toast from the oil and drain on paper towels. Serve hot with dipping bowls of Sweet Cilantro Sauce (page 16) or Quick Sweet and Sour Sauce (page 17).

Shrimp Ball Skewers

These shrimp balls can be steamed or deep-fried.

1 lb (500 g) jumbo shrimp (or tiger prawns), peeled and deveined

2 cloves garlic

3 teaspoons grated fresh ginger

2 teaspoons fish sauce

$1/_4$ teaspoon salt

4 tablespoons cornstarch, plus extra for coating

4 green onions, coarsely chopped

2 tablespoons finely chopped canned water chestnuts

$1/_4$ cup (60 g) finely chopped canned bamboo shoots

Oil, for deep-frying

Lime wedges, to serve

Lime and Fish Sauce (page 17), for dipping

Makes 20 shrimp balls

1 Prepare the Lime and Fish Sauce as instructed on page 17.

2 Process the shrimp, garlic, ginger, fish sauce, salt and cornstarch until smooth in a food processor. Transfer to a bowl and stir in the chopped green onion, water chestnut and bamboo shoot. Using wet hands, mix until well blended.

3 Coat your hands in the cornstarch, spoon 2 tablespoons of the shrimp mixture and shape it into a ball. Toss the shrimp ball in the cornstarch, shaking off any excess. Continue to make the shrimp balls in the same manner with the remaining ingredients.

4 Heat the oil in a large wok until it reaches 375 °F (190 °C) on a deep-frying thermometer, or until a small bread cube dropped in the hot oil sizzles and turns golden. Working in batches, deep-fry the shrimp balls until golden, about 2 minutes. Using a slotted spoon, remove the shrimp balls from the oil and drain on paper towels. Serve hot with lime wedges and dipping bowls of Lime and Fish Sauce. The shrimp balls may be threaded onto skewers after cooking.

Seasoned Rice in a Lotus Leaf

5 dried lotus leaves, halved (or banana leaves or aluminum foil)

1¹/₂ cups (300 g) uncooked short-grain rice, washed in a couple of changes of water and drained

4 Chinese dried mushrooms

1 tablespoon oil

2 teaspoons grated fresh ginger

7 oz (200 g) ground chicken

4 oz (125 g) jumbo shrimp (green king prawns), peeled, deveined and finely chopped

2 dried sweet Chinese sausages (*lap cheong*), finely chopped

1 tablespoon soy sauce

1 tablespoon rice wine

1 tablespoon oyster sauce

2 teaspoons cornstarch, mixed with 1 tablespoon water

1 Soak the lotus leaves in hot water until softened, about 15 minutes, and drain. Line a bamboo steamer with parchment (baking paper) and spread the drained rice on top. Cover the steamer. Half fill a medium wok with water (steamer should not touch water) and bring to a boil. Place the steamer over the boiling water and steam until the rice is tender, 25 to 30 minutes, adding more boiling water to the wok when necessary. Remove from the heat, allow the steamed rice to cool and divide into 10 equal portions.

2 In a small bowl, soak the mushrooms in boiling water until softened. Drain and squeeze out extra liquid from the mushrooms. Remove and discard the thick stems, finely chop the caps.

3 Heat the oil in a wok over medium heat. Stir-fry the ginger until aromatic, about 30 seconds. Add the ground chicken and shrimp, and stir-fry until the mixture changes color, about 3 minutes. Add the chopped sausage and mushroom, and stir-fry for 1 minute. Season with the soy sauce, rice wine and oyster sauce, and stir in the cornstarch mixture. Bring the chicken mixture to a boil and stir until the sauce thickens, about 2 minutes. Remove from the heat and allow to cool.

4 Place the leaves on the work surface. Spoon a portion of the rice onto the center of each piece of leaf and top with 1 tablespoon of the chicken mixture. Fold the leaf over to enclose the filling, then fold in the sides and fold up tightly to form a parcel. Secure with a raffia string or twine.

5 Half fill a large wok with water (steamer should not touch water) and bring to a boil. Working in batches, arrange the parcels in a steamer. Cover and place the steamer over the boiling water. Steam for 15 minutes. Remove from the heat, cut open the parcels and serve hot.

Makes 10 parcels

Steamed Rice Balls

1 cup (220 g) uncooked short-grain rice, washed in a couple of changes of water and drained
1 lb (500 g) ground pork
4 green onions, chopped
4 canned water chestnuts, drained and chopped
1 teaspoon sugar
1 teaspoon salt
2 cloves garlic, crushed
2 teaspoons grated fresh ginger
1 teaspoon sesame oil
2 teaspoons soy sauce
2 teaspoons rice wine
Soy sauce or Ginger Soy Dipping Sauce (page 16), for dipping

1 Place the rice in a medium bowl. Cover with cold water and allow to stand for 30 minutes. Drain, spread out onto a paper towel–lined tray and allow to dry.

2 Combine the pork and all the other ingredients except the dipping sauce in a large bowl. Wet your hands and mix the pork mixture until well combined. Divide into 20 equal portions.

3 Line a bamboo steamer with banana leaf or parchment (baking paper). Using wet hands, shape each portion of the pork mixture into a small ball and roll it in the rice until well coated. Continue to make the meatballs in the same manner with the remaining portions.

4 Half fill a medium wok with water (steamer should not touch water) and bring to a boil. Working in batches, arrange the rice balls in the prepared steamer, allowing room for the rice to expand. Cover and place the steamer over the boiling water. Steam for 30 minutes, adding more boiling water to the wok when necessary. Lift the steamer off the wok and carefully remove the cooked rice balls. Serve warm with soy sauce or Ginger Soy Dipping Sauce (page 16).

Makes 20 rice balls

Egg Custard Tarts

Pastry
3 cups (450 g) flour
6 oz (180 g) lard or shortening
5 tablespoons hot water

Filling
3 eggs, beaten
$1/3$ cup (75 g) superfine (caster) sugar
$1^1/_2$ cups (375 ml) milk
Yellow food coloring (optional)

1 To make the Pastry, sift the flour into a bowl. Using your fingertips, rub the lard or shortening into the flour, until the mixture resembles coarse breadcrumbs. Gradually add the hot water and mix to form a firm dough. Turn the dough out onto a floured work surface and knead until smooth. Using a rolling pin, roll out the dough to $1/8$ in (3 mm) thick. Cut the dough into 24 circles using a 3-in (8-cm) round cutter. Line greased tart (patty) pans with the dough circles.
2 To make the Filling, combine all the ingredients in a bowl and beat until smooth. Pour the Filling into the prepared pastry. Bake in a preheated oven at 425 °F (220 °C) for 10 minutes. Reduce the oven temperature to 400 °F (200 °C) and continue baking until the custard is set, 10 to 15 minutes. Remove from the oven and allow to stand for 10 minutes before transferring to a wire rack to cool. Serve cold or chilled.

Makes 24 tarts

Red Bean Paste Buns

2 teaspoons black sesame seeds,
  to garnish

Dough
$1/_4$ cup (60 ml) milk
2 tablespoons water
$1^1/_2$ tablespoons oil
$1^1/_4$ cups (185 g) flour
$1^1/_2$ teaspoons baking powder
4 tablespoons superfine (caster)
  sugar

Filling
$3/_4$ cup (250 g) canned sweet red
  bean paste

Makes 8 buns

1 Make the Dough by combining the milk, water and oil in a small bowl. Sift the flour and baking powder into a mixing bowl and add the sugar, then gradually pour in the milk mixture, mixing to form a soft Dough. Turn out onto a floured work surface and knead until smooth, 1 to 2 minutes. Wrap the Dough in plastic wrap and chill for 1 hour.

2 Roll the Dough into a sausage shape 8 in (20 cm) long. Cut into eight 1-in ($2^1/_2$-cm) pieces and roll each into a ball. Cover with a damp kitchen towel. Working with a piece of Dough at a time, press into a cup shape. Place $1^1/_2$ tablespoons of the red bean paste in the center of the cup-shaped dough. Gather the edges together, twist and seal into a bun. Cover with a damp kitchen towel and continue to make the buns in the same manner with the remaining Dough.

3 Cut out 8 squares of parchment (baking paper) and place the buns, sealed side down, on the paper. Brush the top of each bun with water and sprinkle with black sesame seeds. Half fill a medium wok with water (steamer should not touch water) and bring to a boil. Working in batches, arrange the buns in the steamer, cover and place the steamer over the boiling water. Steam for 20 minutes. Lift the steamer off the wok and carefully remove the buns. Serve warm.

Sweet Lotus Seed Buns

Dough

1$^1/_2$ teaspoons active dry yeast

$^1/_2$ cup (125 ml) warm water

4 tablespoons superfine (caster)
  sugar

1 cup (150 g) flour

$^1/_2$ cup (60 g) self-rising flour

3 teaspoons butter, melted

Filling

$^3/_4$ cup (250 g) canned sweet
  lotus seed paste

Makes 16 buns

1 To make the Dough, in a small bowl, combine the yeast with 2 tablespoons of the warm water, 1 teaspoon of the sugar and 1 teaspoon of the flour. Mix until well combined. Cover with a kitchen towel and allow to stand in a warm place until frothy, about 15 minutes.

2 Sift the remaining flour and self-rising flour into a large bowl. Add the remaining sugar and warm water, butter and the yeast mixture. Using a wooden spoon, mix to form a soft Dough. Turn the Dough out onto a floured work surface and knead until smooth and elastic, 3 to 5 minutes. Place the Dough in a large greased bowl, cover and leave to stand in a warm place until doubled in size, about 1 hour.

3 Punch down the Dough. Turn out onto a floured work surface and knead until smooth, about 5 minutes. Divide the Dough into 16 equal pieces and roll or press out each piece to form a 2$^1/_4$-in (6-cm) circle. Cover the Dough with a damp kitchen towel. Working with a Dough circle at a time, spoon 2 teaspoons of the Filling to the center. Gather the edges together and twist to seal into a bun. Cover with a kitchen towel. Continue to make the buns in the same manner with the remaining Dough.

4 Cut out 16 squares of parchment (baking paper) and place the buns, sealed side down, on the paper. Half fill a medium wok with water (steamer should not touch water) and bring to a boil. Working in batches, arrange the buns in a steamer, cover and place the steamer over the boiling water. Steam for 15 to 20 minutes. Lift the steamer off the wok and carefully remove the buns. Serve warm.

Mango Pudding

4 ripe mangoes, peeled and pitted
4 tablespoons orange juice
1 cup (250 ml) water
$1/_3$ cup (75 g) superfine (caster)
  sugar
6 teaspoons gelatin powder
Mango slices, to garnish

1 Process the mango and orange juice in a food processor until smooth. Strain through a coarse sieve and set aside.
2 Combine the water, sugar and gelatin in a saucepan. Stir over low heat until the sugar and gelatin dissolve. Remove from the heat and allow to cool for 5 minutes. Stir in the processed mango and mix well. Pour into 6 serving glasses or 6 individual jelly molds. Refrigerate until firm, 2 to 3 hours. If in molds, invert onto serving plates. Serve, garnished with mango slices.

Serves 6

Mango Almond Pudding

2 cups (500 ml) cold water
$1/_3$ cup (75 g) superfine (caster) sugar
5 teaspoons gelatin powder
$2/_3$ cup (150 ml) evaporated milk
$1/_2$ teaspoon almond extract
Mango slices, to serve

Place the water and sugar in a saucepan. Sprinkle the gelatin over the top. Bring the mixture to a boil, stirring for 1 minute. Remove from the heat. Add the milk and almond extract, and mix well. Pour into a greased pan about $7^1/_2$ x 11 in (19 x 28 cm). Refrigerate until firm, 2 to 3 hours. Cut into small pieces and serve with slices of fresh mango.

Makes about 16 pieces

Sweet Coconut Rice Bars

2¹/₂ cups (550 g) uncooked glutinous rice
2¹/₄ cups (560 ml) thick coconut
milk (see note)
¹/₂ cup (110 g) superfine (caster)
sugar

Topping
1¹/₄ cups (150 g) unsweetened
dried shredded coconut
¹/₄ cup (60 ml) thick coconut
milk, warmed
¹/₂ cup (90 g) shaved palm sugar
or dark brown sugar
3 tablespoons water

Makes about 20 pieces

1 Place the glutinous rice in a large bowl and cover
with cold water. Allow to stand overnight, then
drained. Line a large bamboo steamer with parchment
(baking paper) and spread the drained rice on top.
Cover the steamer. Half fill a medium wok with water
(steamer should not touch water) and bring to a boil.
Place the steamer over the boiling water and steam
until the rice is tender and cooked, about 45 minutes,
adding more boiling water to the wok when necessary.
2 Place the steamed rice in a medium, heavy-bottomed
saucepan. Add the thick coconut milk and sugar, and
stir over low heat until the coconut milk has been
absorbed, about 10 minutes. Evenly spread the rice into
a shallow baking pan (about 7¹/₂ x 11 in/19 x 28 cm)
lined with parchment (baking paper). Refrigerate until
firm, about 2 hours.
3 To make the Topping, combine the shredded coconut
and coconut milk in a bowl. In a small saucepan, combine the palm sugar or dark brown sugar and water,
and stir over low heat until the mixture thickens slightly,
3 to 4 minutes. Remove from the heat and pour into
the coconut mixture and stir until well combined.
Allow to cool to room temperature.
4 Spread the Topping over the rice and return to chill
for 1 hour. Cut into small squares to serve.

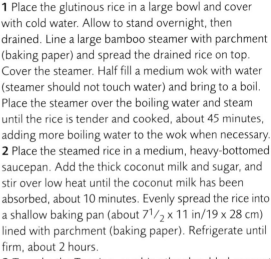

Note: Coconut milk is the milky white cooking base
derived from the flesh of a mature coconut. While freshly
pressed milk has more flavor, coconut cream and milk are
now widely sold in cans and packets that are quick and
convenient. You can add 1 cup of water to 1 cup of
canned or packet coconut cream to obtain thick coconut
milk. Canned or packet coconut cream and milk comes in
varying consistencies depending on the brand, and you
will need to try them out and adjust the thickness by
adding water as needed.

Complete List of Recipes